An Instinct

By Hugo Timbrell

methuen | drama
LONDON · NEW YORK · OXFORD · NEW DELHI · SYDNEY

METHUEN DRAMA
Bloomsbury Publishing Plc
50 Bedford Square, London, WC1B 3DP, UK
1359 Broadway, New York, NY 10018, USA
29 Earlsfort Terrace, Dublin 2, Ireland

BLOOMSBURY, METHUEN DRAMA and the Methuen
Drama logo are trademarks of Bloomsbury Publishing Plc

First published in Great Britain 2025

Copyright © Hugo Timbrell, 2025

Hugo Timbrell has asserted their right under the Copyright, Designs and Patents Act, 1988, to be identified as Author of this work.

For legal purposes the Acknowledgements on p. vii constitute an extension of this copyright page.

Cover design: Carrie Croft
Cover image: Carrie Croft

All rights reserved. No part of this publication may be: i) reproduced or transmitted in any form, electronic or mechanical, including photocopying, recording or by means of any information storage or retrieval system without prior permission in writing from the publishers; or ii) used or reproduced in any way for the training, development or operation of artificial intelligence (AI) technologies, including generative AI technologies. The rights holders expressly reserve this publication from the text and data mining exception as per Article 4(3) of the Digital Single Market Directive (EU) 2019/790.

Bloomsbury Publishing Plc does not have any control over, or responsibility for, any third-party websites referred to or in this book. All internet addresses given in this book were correct at the time of going to press. The author and publisher regret any inconvenience caused if addresses have changed or sites have ceased to exist, but can accept no responsibility for any such changes.

No rights in incidental music or songs contained in the work are hereby granted and performance rights for any performance/presentation whatsoever must be obtained from the respective copyright owners.

All rights whatsoever in this play are strictly reserved and application for performance etc. should be made before rehearsals begin to the author via Bloomsbury Publishing, performance.permissions@bloomsbury.com.
No performance may be given unless a licence has been obtained.

A catalogue record for this book is available from the British Library.

A catalog record for this book is available from the Library of Congress.

ISBN:	PB:	978-1-3506-0634-0
	ePDF:	978-1-3506-0635-7
	eBook:	978-1-3506-0636-4

Series: Modern Plays

Typeset by Westchester Publishing Services
Printed and bound in Great Britain

To find out more about our authors and books
visit www.bloomsbury.com and sign up for our newsletters.

An Instinct

By Hugo Timbrell

For Dad

Creative Team

HUGO TIMBRELL Writer

Hugo is a queer, dyslexic, Bruntwood Prize-longlisted writer from London interested in stories with great plots, interesting forms and things that make you laugh.

He was part of Hampstead Theatre's invitation-only INSPIRE writers' programme 2023/24, led by award-winning playwright Roy Williams. He was a writer-on-attachment at the Traverse Theatre, Edinburgh during 2019. His work has been developed and supported by organisations including Traverse Theatre, Hampstead Theatre, Bruntwood Prize, Selladoor, Omnibus Theatre, HighTide Theatre, Park Theatre and Arcola Theatre. Credits include *My Life as a Cowboy* (Omnibus Theatre, 2024); *The Vessel* (Hampstead Theatre INSPIRE 2023/24); *An Instinct* (Theatre503 International Playwriting Award 2023 Shortlist); *My Life as a Cowboy* (Park Theatre, 2022); *The Job Interview* (Sell a Door, 2021); *Motherland* (Traverse Theatre, 2019) and *Death Metal Band* (Bruntwood Prize for Playwriting 2019 Longlist).

LUCY FOSTER Director

Lucy Foster is a writer and director interested in unique narratives in ambitious and unexpected genres. She is represented by Jennifer Thomas at United Agents.

Recent projects for theatre include a commission for Chronic Insanity digital theatre platform Fablemosh with creepypasta horror play *Cuckoo's Corner*; development of new dark thriller play *How to Kill Your Darlings* (co-written with Jon Barton) with Chalk Line Theatre; commission with Hampstead Theatre; a Bush Theatre allotment for a new horror play and two commissions as part of the Write the Girl scheme for 14–18 year old girls. She's been shortlisted for the Verity Bargate Award, Theatre503 International Playwriting Prize, and in 2019 she won the Alpine Fellowship Theatre Prize. As a director, she's worked at venues such as Park Theatre and Trafalgar Studios and she's been Offie-nominated as Best Director.

For screen, Lucy is currently developing her first horror feature, feminist folk horror *Huldra*, with Boudica Entertainment; she's written two made-for-TV thrillers with Reel One Entertainment; she's developing a new comedy TV series *Ego Warriors* with Climate Spring Productions; and she directed her first two short films in 2023. Her short film *Santa's Little Helper* (produced by Crossroad Pictures) premiered at Dead Northern festival 2025. She was also selected for the Frightfest 2023 New Blood Class for her feminist horror feature, *Headless Chicks*.

CROFT & DYE PRODUCTIONS Producer

Croft & Dye Productions are partners in both producing and general management.

Having worked separately in the industry, we decided to bring our skill sets together so that we could continue to provide the kind of outstanding services that we are known for individually but on a much larger scale.

Founded by two award-winning producers and experienced general managers, C&D Productions specialises in stage new, high-quality, dynamic work. Providing the outstanding general management services that they are known for individually. To be meaningful champions of stories that should be shown on stage. Theatre should be exciting. Because without that excitement, without that magic of space and time and focus, then everything stops working. We believe that if you're truly passionate about what you do, then it's almost impossible not to change the world around you.

As a company, Croft & Dye Production's current credits include *By Their Fruits* (Theatre503, 2024); the critically acclaimed *Julie: The Musical* (The Other Palace, 2024) and the five-star premiere of *Foam* (Finborough Theatre, 2024; winner of Best Production 2024 at London Pub Theatre awards) and an R&D of new musical *Windsong* (The Other Palace, 2024 and Seven Dials Playhouse, 2025).

KIT HINCHCLIFFE Set and Costume Design

Kit trained at Central Saint Martins College of Art and Design. Since graduating, her work has spanned theatre, dance and installation.

She is co-artistic director of Lidless Theatre and regularly collaborates with Architecture Social Club as designer/fabricator.

Work includes *The Poltigist* (Arcola Theatre); *The Pitch Fork Disney* (Kings Head Theatre); *Dear Martin* (Arcola Theatre); *Tarantula* (Arcola Theatre); *Miss Julie* (Park Theatre), *Copper Beaches* (Corbett Theatre); *Leaves of Glass* (Park Theatre); *Oresteia* (Corbett Theatre); *The Journey to Venice* (Finborough Theatre); *The Poltergeist* (Arcola Theatre); *Camino Real* and *Cymbeline* (Bridewell Theatre); *Mapping Gender* (Baltic Centre for Contemporary Art, Cambridge Junction and The Place); *A Hideous Monstrous Verminous Creature* (The Place); *La Bohème* (King's Head Theatre); *Boys* (Barbican Centre); *Festen* (Corbett Theatre); *Tender Napalm* (King's Head Theatre); *Well Lit* (Dansstationen Malmö and The Place); *Moonfleece* (Pleasance); *Pebbles* (Katzpace); *Heroes* (Bridge House Theatre); *Beetles from the West* (Hope Theatre); *Fundamentals* (Platform TheatreKX).

CAELAN ORAM Lighting Design

Caelan (they/them) is a London based technician, currently working full time in the Lighting Resources department of the National Theatre. They are an MA graduate from Guildhall School of Music and Drama, where they studied Theatre Production and Design. Also a freelance lighting designer and technician, Caelan has worked at venues across London, including VAULT Festival, The Almeida, Theatre Royal Stratford East and Greenwich Theatre. Caelan is interested in working with bold new theatre, especially exploring themes of queerness, marginalised identity and community.

Recent credits include *A Manchester Anthem* (Riverside Studios, 2025, Hope Mill Theatre, 2025, Edinburgh Fringe, 2023, VAULT Festival, 2023), *Drag Baby* (Pleasance London, 2024); *I F*cked You In My Spaceship* (VAULT Festival 2023).

JULIAN STARR Sound Design

Julian studied at the National Institute of Dramatic Arts (NIDA), was detailed in Australia's *Stage Whispers* as one of the Top 4 Sound Designer and Composers in Australia and is currently the associate sound designer at the Finborough Theatre.

Recent sound design work includes *Four Play* (King's Head Theatre); *Echo* (King's Head Theatre); *Seagull: True Story* (Marylebone Theatre); *The Wanderers* (Marylebone Theatre); *This Bitter Earth* (Soho Theatre); *Diagnosis* (Finborough Theatre); *Dear Martin* (Arcola Theatre); *Acid's Reign* (Pleasance Theatre); *Miracle on 34th Street* (HOME Manchester); *The River* (Greenwich Theatre); *The End* (Bush Theatre); *Bombay Superstars* (UK tour); *23.5 Hours* (Park Theatre); *F**king Men* (Waterloo East); *The Picture of Dorian Gray* (Associate Sound Designer –, Theatre Royal Haymarket); *Sharon Osbourne – Cut The Crap!* (Fortune Theatre); *The White Factory* (Marylebone Theatre – Offie Nomination for Best Sound Design); *Miss Peony* (Australian tour); *Song From Far Away* (HOME Manchester, Hampstead Theatre and BBC Radio 4); *ZOG* (West End and UK tour); *Rose* (West End, Hope Mill, Park Theatre – Offie Nominated for Best Sound Design); *Return to the Dirt (*Queensland Theatre Company); *Animal* (Park Theatre and UK tour); *Sleepwalking* (Hampstead Theatre); *Scrounger* (Finborough Theatre – Offie Nomination for Best Sound Design); *The Dwarfs* (White Bear Theatre – Offie Nomination for Best Sound Design) and *Aisha* (Tristan Bates – Offie Nomination Best Sound Design).

CUP OF AMBITION Marketing

Founded in 2020, female-led marketing collective Cup of Ambition champions projects that are big in aspiration: from fringe theatre to main stages and everything in between. Their client base includes both commercial and Off-West End work, UK tours, in-house marketing support and consultancy for venues, Edinburgh Fringe shows, festivals and live events, and more. Past successes include working with immersive industry leaders Punchdrunk on *The Burnt City* (2023), managing the initial and returning runs of sell-out smash hit new musical *Cable Street* (2024), and helping to open the new King's Head venue in Angel, North London (2024). Alongside managing shows and projects, they also consult on overall comms strategies and offer in-house consultancy and support to venues and festivals across the UK and internationally, and support transfers of work from the US and Australia in finding London audiences.

CHLOÉ NELKIN CONSULTING PR

Founded in 2010, Chloé Nelkin Consulting is a well-regarded arts and theatre PR agency with a wide and successful reach and close connections with the press. With over fifteen years' experience, CNC has delivered high-profile and successful campaigns including West End productions, high-profile galas, Off-West End shows, touring theatre and Edinburgh Fringe productions. CNC is led by founder Chloé Nelkin. The company is also responsible for The Pink Podcast, CNC Books and CNC Live.

Cast

CONOR DUMBRELL Max

Conor Dumbrell (he/him) is an actor and writer who trained at LAMDA. Theatre credits include *Four Felons and a Funeral* (Birmingham Hippodrome and UK tour); *Crying Shame* (Pleasance and Stanley Arts); *Instructions* (Summerhall); *George* (Omnibus); *I Hate It Here* (UK tour); *The Snow Queen* and *Crackers* (Polka); *Bleak Expectations* (West End); *Insides* (Pleasance). Screen and audio credits include *The Last Hurrah*, *Rubinov*, *Revenge is a Dish*, *Beans on Toast* and *GUTS*. Conor is a Platform Resident Artist at Artsdepot and co-director of award-winning theatre company Sweet Beef.

JOE WALSHAM Tom

Joe is a Bromley-born actor and filmmaker, shaped by a lifelong love of films. He trained at Rose Bruford College, where he discovered a natural pull toward characters who meet the world with curiosity and openness—qualities he brings to every role. Joe's screen credits include the Sky TV series *That Hidden Camera Family* and the short film *Better Safe Than Sorry*. On stage, he has performed at the Unicorn Theatre in *Boudica* and made his West End debut as a child in *Oliver!* Joe can usually be found in the cinema. His dream role? Any character in an action film who gets a dubbed-over Wilhelm scream.

BEN NORRIS Charlie

Ben Norris is an actor, poet, theatre-maker and film-maker.

He co-created and starred in the Olivier-nominated West End musical *The Choir of Man*, and is the voice of Ben Archer in *The Archers* on BBC Radio 4 and Rogier in the videogame *Elden Ring*.

His latest short film, *Toad in the Hole*, screened at London Film Festival 2025. His previous short, *Monitor*, was commissioned by the BBC and is now on Short of the Week, and his first, *Send Her Victorious,* was nominated for a Royal Television Society Award. Ben's debut solo show, *The Hitchhiker's Guide to the Family*, won the IdeasTap Underbelly Award and toured the UK and Australia from 2015–2018, including a run at the Southbank Centre. His first play, *Autopilot*, was named by The Stage as one of the shows of the year at the 2022 Edinburgh Fringe.

Other theatre credits include *The Pianist* (Southampton Mayflower); *A Leap in the Dark* (New Vic); *A Short Tour of the Heart* (Nottingham Playhouse/Theatr Clwyd); *Shootout* (White Bear); *I'm Just Here to Buy Soy Sauce* (Theatre503); *E15* (Pleasance).

Television and film credits include *Suspect* (Disney+); *Hard Cracked The Wind* (Early Day Films); *Send Her Victorious* (Channel 4); *Super Citrus Force* (Channel 4); *Chronos* (Frokost Film).

Other radio credits include *Lola vs Powerman, Arthur, The Wall, Portrait of the Artist, The Liquid You* (all BBC Radio 4); *Spitfire* (BBC World Service).

Ben is a current associate artist at Lincoln Arts Centre and has been a writer in residence at Theatr Clwyd and a creative associate at Nottingham Playhouse. He has written commissions for BBC Radio 4 and the Royal Festival Hall, among others, and has published two pamphlets of poetry.

He trained at the Royal Welsh College of Music and Drama.

An Instinct

By Hugo Timbrell

Setting

England.

A forest. Off a motorway.

A cabin in the woods *(kinda like the film but less Hammer Horror – or is it?) – it could be full wooden attire – tables, chairs, curtains, a wood burner, a bench with horse heads carved into the armrests (but these could all just be gestured to) – it is rustic though, not modern – there is the bedroom offstage and a kitchen offstage in another direction – failing that, all that is really required is a 'window', a 'front door' and, most importantly, an axe.*

Characters

Max – *thirties – a real Gemini – fun – torn – anxious – and easily led.*

Tom – *thirties – a real Capricorn – likes things by the books – runs a successful consultancy business (whatever that means) and has two pairs of glasses that he's had exclusively for the past ten years.*

Charlie – *thirties – a real Aries – brutish – often sweaty – erratic – fast-paced and primal.*

Note

For actors, directors, readers, and everyone in between – **slow and steady wins the race**.

' - ' is a break in thought.

' – ' is an interrupted sentence.

Scene One

The Cabin. Night.

Tom *stands there with their luggage.*

Max Your parents - sorry *your* parents own *this* place

Tom Well I know it's a bit rustic

Max *This* is theirs?

Tom A bit dusty and - no one lives here on a day to day basis so there's going to be dust - probably a few spiders too if you look hard enough

Max Cheryl and Nigel bought this?

Tom Correct

Max *looks around and it doesn't compute.*

Max When?

Tom They like remoteness - sometimes

Max They like the Costa del Sol - they like that - not the Forest of, bloody, Dean

Tom Or at least they liked the idea of it

Pause.

Tom *puts down their bags.*

He goes to shut the front door.

He starts to unpack.

Max *stays put – unsure of what to do.*

He's still looking around, sussing the place out, checking for dust.

Max Never told me they had somewhere like this

Tom It never came up

Max When you think of England you don't think rickety old cabin in the woods - you think lodge in a forest - with a hot tub - Center Parcs

Tom It was actually quite expensive this place

Max *is astonished by this.*

Max Really?

Tom Not my fault it never came up - you never asked

Tom *goes over to the wood burner, shivering.*

He starts to work out how to put the wood burner on.

Max I knew your parents quite well at one point you know

Tom You did

Max We went on a few holidays - in the sun - Cheryl and I loved an Aperol spritz by the pool of an afternoon - Nigel in his Speedos

Tom Yeah

Max Good times

Tom *gives* **Max** *a look.*

Max Not your dad in Speedos - your mum with the Aperol spritz

Pause.

Tom The logs here don't look good

Max There's no heating?

Tom It's a cabin –

Max Wi-Fi?

Tom A cabin in the woods

Pause.

Max Right I'm suddenly having - sorry - maybe I shouldn't be here

Tom You can survive without Wi-Fi trust me

Max Yes but it's suddenly dawning on me

Tom And we're here now aren't we - we've driven all this way

Max This might have been a mistake

Tom We won't talk about the past - I promise

Pause.

Max *sits down.*

He watches **Tom** *try and get the fire working.*

Max So where are your parents?

Tom At home

Max They aren't coming here?

Tom Well - no

Max You didn't think they might want to come with us?

Tom I think they would have been uncomfortable

Max But we've been on holiday before

Tom Holiday?

Max I mean we were quite close at one point

Tom *stops what he is doing.*

Tom I left them

Pause.

Max Oh

Tom Yeah - well yeah I had to leave them because there wasn't enough –

Max Sorry I - sorry the way you said that sounded quite severe

Tom They're stuck in the city now so

Pause.

Tom It's OK

Tom *gets back to work.*

Max *stands up and starts pacing.*

Max Sorry I'm just a bit - I can see you're worried but there's no need to be they'll be fine

Tom Stressed - I can see that

Max Stressed and well I just really didn't expect my week to go like this –

Tom It all sort of spiralled didn't it –

Max The week started at the office with Nina's - sorry Sarah from finance's birthday cake –

Tom We had to plan quick or - oh it was Sarah's birthday was it –

Max Then some news announcements and well that was pretty scary and –

Tom It doesn't look good

Max So I hope you don't mind that I called you up?

Tom I didn't

Max My parents are the other side of the country and Charlie –

Tom I was always going to say yes

Max You know otherwise I would have tried to make it to my parents

Pause.

Tom With all the stuff I had packed for us there wasn't enough space for mine –

Max And then suddenly I'm in my ex-boyfriend's car flying down the motorway to a cabin in the woods - Jesus now I say it like that this all sounds a little bit mental

Pause.

Tom *stops again.*

Tom I left my parents behind - Jesus

Max What did Cheryl say?

Tom Well she cried - obviously

Max Right

Tom Tears streaming down her face actually

Max I know she's sensitive

Tom Blubbing - really going for it yeah

Max She loves you

Tom But I told her - you want us to survive - you want us to survive don't you? I'm the one with all the genes and you want the genes to survive this don't you? And so she nodded - and I said good and hugged her and patted her on the head and she proper snotted on my shirt from all the crying - which was actually pretty disgusting - then I got in my car and drove off to pick you up

Pause.

Max Hang on - you're thinking of having a child now?

Tom That's what you took from what I've just said?

Max You're now - sorry - do you want kids now?

Tom Well not in the cabin no

Max A woman?

Tom No - well yes a woman - but no - by myself - not by myself because that's impossible - we're not big fat huge amoebas

8   An Instinct

Max   When?

Tom   Soon - I've been looking into it - clocks are ticking

Pause.

Max   This is a lot of new information to process - I'm in the middle of nowhere with my ex and he's just said he's going to be a father

Tom   Not yet

Max   Well clocks are ticking

Tom   We haven't been together for nearly a year now

Max   But I just didn't expect there to suddenly be a baby in your life

Tom   There's not

Max   Yes but in theory there could be - I mean there could be at some point that's what you're saying you know –

Tom   You broke up with me

Pause.

Sorry I know I said we wouldn't –

Max   Just - give me a minute

Pause.

Tom   I didn't think you'd already be acting this way

Max   Acting what way?

Tom   Well you're a bit flappy

Max   Flappy?

Tom   Yeah flappy you know

Tom *flaps his arms like a bird.*

Max   Don't do that

Tom   What?

Max I'm not the only camp one here

Tom Flustered that's what I meant

Max So I'm flappy you're right I am flappy

Tom It's only the first day of this so I think you need to breathe a bit

Max I hadn't factored in that you had –

Tom Things have changed - life has changed –

Max That you'd moved on

Pause.

Tom I've grown yeah - I've changed so

Max I know it's just - well it's - it's good to see

The wind suddenly bangs against the doors and windows.

Max Christ

Tom Just the wind - the cabin sort of juts out on a hill so –

Max This is pretty remote isn't it - hard to tell cos it's so dark –

Pause.

Max I don't really know where we are actually so

Tom We can lock ourselves in and really well - nobody will ever know we're here

Pause.

Max *looks around the cabin again.*

Max Well maybe this is - well actually all quite exciting

Tom You're excited?

Max I am

Tom A minute ago you were almost hyperventilating

Max Well I've changed my mind

Tom OK - good

Max You know this is quite 'Escape to the Country'

Tom I'm glad you're getting into the spirit of things I suppose

Max Something quite masculine about this cabin - although I'm not that sort of person you know

Tom We're not some of those masc for masc types

Max We're not vain –

Tom Not stereotypes no

They look awkward for a moment.

Max So we camp out here then - until this all blows over

Tom I've got us what we need yeah - board games too

Max We can get updates on our phones to see how it's going

Tom I left my phone in the city - they rot your brain

Max Well I've got mine

Tom I think you would be hard pressed to find signal here

Max *gets out his phone.*

There's no signal.

He goes over to another side of the room.

Still no signal.

He raises his phone as high up into a corner as possible.

There's still no signal.

Max But I haven't - told anyone where I am or - I waited until we got here –

Tom Too late - sorry - but don't worry or anything

Pause.

It starts to dawn on **Max**.

Max So just you and me

Tom Yeah

Max Stuck here with my ex-boyfriend

Tom Well don't sound so upset - you asked me

Max I'm not upset - it's just –

Tom Intense - yeah I feel that too

Pause.

Max What's the axe for?

Tom To chop your head off

Tom *laughs.*

Max *doesn't.*

Tom The wood burner

Max Now that is masculine

Max *goes over and picks up the axe – looking it over.*

Max This is like back in time - I mean - Cheryl loves her central heating, used to blame her for global warming, that's why I still can't get my head around this

Tom It's just a cabin in a forest - you might like it

Pause.

An idea occurs to **Max**.

Max I kinda wanna go and chop some wood now –

Tom It's night-time

Max And you can judge me all you want but I'm going to be taking photos of myself chopping wood with my top off as some sort of memento of this place –

Tom Don't be that gay

12 An Instinct

Max A holiday kinda photo you know might as well make the most of it

Tom You've no internet to post it anyway

Max *rolls his eyes.*

He goes towards the front door.

Tom *stops him.*

A stand-off.

Tom Max stop for a second - now listen - I know this might come as a shock to you - but we're gonna be here for quite a while - I can't tell you how long - but it's going to be quite a long time - and - I know you're not panicked anymore so I don't want to scare you or anything - but this is going to get bad - very bad - for a long time - until it gets better again

Max Sorry I'm a bit lost - I don't quite follow –

Tom This virus - it's a lot - it's going to be a lot for people and it's going to get quite scary

Max It's a flu –

Tom It's going to get bad - from what I've heard there are going to be a significant number of people who will die - in the cities - which is why we've come here - why you called me up - so we can wait out the storm

Pause.

Max How do you know?

Tom I've been studying it for a while

Max Online articles are just clickbait - I used to tell you that before

Tom I know you think I'm a hypochondriac

Max You are

Scene One   13

Tom   They're closing the city off –

Max   For a bit - you know as sort of - well I thought about this like a little retreat in all the madness

Tom   No one in or out - no one leaving and no one going anywhere - for a long time

Max *laughs, an uncomfortable 'can't believe it' laugh.*

Tom   I think your body was telling you something - when you felt so panicked on the way here - because I think you already know this is going to get bad - and that's why you came here - without telling anyone - without provisions or supplies - with your ex-boyfriend - you followed your instincts

Max *takes this in.*

Tom   We'll just need time to adjust

Max   What about *my* parents?

Tom   I know

Max   My job?

Tom   Don't worry too much about that now

Max   Charlie?

Pause.

Maybe I should - yes yes I should - I should be with them really

Tom   The city - the roads - they shut down tonight - your parents will be safer without you around trust me - we all might already have it - and you might give it to someone near them or even one of them

Pause.

Max   Then Charlie

Tom   Doesn't he have a camper van or something?

Max What's that got to do with anything?

Tom He has options is what I mean

Max I think I should be with my partner right?

Tom Max I think there's a reason why Charlie was on the bottom of your list just then - but I think he might top the list of reasons why you came here with me

Max *goes to leave.*

But **Tom** *stops him.*

Tom You can't drive

Max I'll walk

Tom Sorry I can't - it's for your own good - trust me

Pause.

A stand-off.

Max It's scary - I didn't know what to do - so I came here with you

Max *goes to sit down.*

Tom I'll go out to chop wood - and I'll go to the local shop - but other than that

Max Well I'll come with you

Tom They won't like outsiders –

Max They're not feral

Tom Rural

Max You make it sound like the locals are dangerous

Pause.

Are the locals dangerous?

Tom Some of the people round here know me - and I know them - they're proud and sometimes quite aggressive - they can get quite suspicious of outsiders and foreigners and stuff like that - they're that sort of crowd - we have to be as much on the down low as possible

Tom *goes back to the wood burner.*

Max *is taking this all in.*

Max So what you're saying is - what so you're saying that I can't leave this cabin?

The wood burner starts working.

Tom I'm saying we're going to survive this

The wind suddenly blows hard and fast again and rattles the doors and windows.

We're going to survive this together

Scene Two

The Cabin. Three weeks later. Afternoon.

Max *is alone, reading.*

He's bored. Very, very bored.

The wind is blowing hard at the door and the window. You can hear it through the leaves.

Max *looks towards the door.*

Max *goes back to reading.*

The wind howls even harder now.

Max *looks towards it.*

He then closes his book and throws it across the room.

He sighs.

He stands up.

He stretches up to the sky, and bends over, to start a sun salutation.

He gets bored midway through and stops.

He lies there on the floor for a while and stares up towards the ceiling.

He lets out a huge sigh.

He goes to the door.

The wind howls against it again.

He slowly goes to open the door.

He breathes in the fresh air.

We hear birds in the trees.

He lets out a sigh – but he's content.

Scene Two

Suddenly, a man in an industrial gas mask and full hazmat suit jumps up from around the door.

Max *screams in terror.*

Max *rushes to a corner in the room.*

The man in the gas mask comes in holding the axe and some shopping.

Max *screams again.*

The man shuts the door as quickly as possible.

He drops the shopping and it goes everywhere.

The man turns around and takes off his mask.

It is **Tom**.

Tom What did I say?

Max No - no no - no no - Jesus Christ no

Tom What did I specifically tell you not to do?

Max I'm going to - oh my god I think I'm - my heart is going to fall out of my arse

Tom There was one rule - stay inside

Max Like it's just going to burst out of me

Tom You could have killed yourself

Pause.

Max *I* could have killed myself? Me? *I* could have

Tom You could have killed both of us

Max You're the one who has just snuck up on me –

Tom No I didn't sneak –

Max Dressed up like they're going to a zombie apocalypse –

Tom I don't sneak that's not what I do - let me get that straight –

Max Looking like someone going to some weird fetish party in Berlin

Pause.

Max *breathes.*

Tom *goes to put the axe down in the corner.*

They start to simmer down.

Tom Look OK - you'd been doing so well - three weeks of doing this - I understand it's tough - a real will power thing - but we have to stick to it - it's for our own good

Max OK - right OK I've calmed down now - right so - first off - why in the actual fuck are you wearing that?

Tom I don't want to panic or frighten you –

Max Well it's a bit too late for that Tom isn't it

Tom You'd been sleeping in late, so you didn't get a chance to see me in my new gear this morning

Max There's not much else to do but sleep

Tom You'd been doing so well up until this point

Max Stop saying that I don't know what you mean

Tom With this - being locked in here - not locked - three weeks - you'd done so well - and you could have ruined it

Pause.

Max I've finished all the puzzles - I've cleaned the entire cabin as best I could - I've planned every meal we've attempted to cook on that stove –

Tom I'm so grateful for that

Max I've baked banana bread - three times - fucking banana bread –

Tom You're tense still

Scene Two 19

Max But after all that - I now feel like I'm going to go mad

Pause.

Tom OK I need you to get a hold of yourself

Max *Me* get a hold of myself

Tom To see the bigger picture

Max This whole set up is unfair

Tom Unfair?

Max You go to get us supplies - you go outside and chop wood - you spend a lot of time outside actually and –

Tom We've talked about the wood chopping

Max I'm not talking about the photos

Tom I'm the one that goes outside and –

Max And I'm stuck in here –

Tom I'm the one that could die - everyday - I risk my life - for you - everyday

Pause.

Max Listen I know you didn't want me going outside because of the neighbours but –

Tom The neighbours are agitated - actually - last night the local supermarket was looted

Max Shit

Pause.

Tom And all you think about is how unfair you've got it here

Max Sorry but - I really didn't think you'd have this kind of reaction about opening a door

Pause.

20   An Instinct

They stare at each other.

What?

Tom   You're stupid really aren't you - you know you're just –

Max   I'm not

Tom   Why do you think I'm wearing this?

Max   Well I asked you why and you didn't tell me

Tom   The virus has changed

Pause.

I told you things would be bad

Max   Well how am I supposed to know if it's changed?

Tom   The wind - the air - the virus - it's really contagious and - it's changed –

Max   How do you know this?

Tom   You don't trust me?

Max   Where have you got this information from?

Tom   I've seen it in town - people are dressing exactly how I am

Pause.

The way the virus spreads - it's in the air - on the wind

Pause.

This starts to sink in.

Max   So I won't open the door then

Tom   No

Max   And the suit is

Tom   The best shot I have of not getting it

Scene Two

They stare at each other.

Something thuds at the door.

Max What the fuck was that?

Tom Stay there

Tom *goes over to get the axe.*

He puts the mask back on.

He opens the door, steps outside and disappears.

Pause.

Tom *comes back in with a dead bird in his hands – he shuts the door behind him.*

Tom It looks like a bird?

Max Well is it still alive?

Tom I'm not sure

Pause.

Listen I think we're just both stressed by the intensity of all this - I honestly think this is all just stress you know? If we just forget about just now and just - why don't I try and make us something to eat instead

Tom *goes to pick up the shopping strewn all over the floor.*

Max The disinfectant is in the kitchen

Tom Right

Tom *goes towards the kitchen – but stops when* **Max** *speaks.*

Max You know - I have to say - I really don't appreciate - please don't call me stupid - OK?

Pause.

Tom Grow up

Max What?

Tom I'm risking my life here - for both of us

Max I understand but when you called me stupid –

Tom All you have to do is stay in here - and potter - potter about - and you can't even seem to manage that - while I'm out there risking my life - you know what when we were together - you were just like this - you were just as selfish as you are now

Tom *takes the shopping to the kitchen and exits.*

Max *stands there, alone, thinking about what has just happened.*

Pause.

Max OK Tom - I'm - I'm sorry about the door

Pause.

Tom *comes back in.*

They look at each other.

Tom I suppose you didn't know about how it's changed

Max I won't open it again

Pause.

Tom We need to limit how much contact we have with the outside - the locals are - we need to keep our heads down - we don't want to be caught up in that - it's best that as little people know we're here as possible

Pause.

Max I appreciate what you've done for me

Pause.

I'm sorry that you think - I'm sorry that you think I'm selfish

Tom It's OK

Max But I'm not selfish - I'm not being selfish

Tom   This is exactly what ended us

Max   OK maybe let's not talk about that

Tom   Why not?

Max   Because that's in the past

Tom   It's always about you - about what you want - about how you are - everything is always and will always be about you Max

Pause.

Max   All I did was open a door to get some fresh air

Tom   So you're not sorry then

Max   I've been locked up here

Tom   You still don't get it do you

Max   Stop talking to me like I'm stupid

Tom   I had plans for us - I had already imagined a whole future - for us - and it was thrown back in my face - I gave you lots didn't I - I mean I looked after you and - and all for what?

Pause.

Max   You make out like I'm some selfish monster or something –

Tom   You left me for Charlie - because what? He's constantly a bit sweaty and looks the part - after all I did for you - and look at me now - still trying to help you

Max   Can we - please

Tom   You're wrong we haven't properly spoken about this you know

Max   OK but - now? In the middle of all this - I mean I really am sorry about the door –

Tom   Even now you don't take it seriously

Pause.

When I found out about it - I'm quite a rational person - but it felt like someone had sucked something out of my torso - and my whole chest was just this vacuum - and then weeks later someone put cement right into the cavity and it hardened - and I just sank

Pause.

Max OK we're in a stressful situation here

Tom I've never spoken to you about it because I didn't want to make you feel bad - but I felt so bad - so bad for such a long time

Max Our relationship wasn't perfect Tom

Pause.

Tom Was it worth it?

Max I love Charlie

Tom I've heard - I knew he was a brute - you can tell

Max I don't know what you've heard but –

Tom I wouldn't hit you - I would never have hit you - you know that?

Max Charlie's complicated - he's been stressed - he thinks someone is stalking us - he gets agitated –

Pause.

Listen I don't want you to feel bad here - I don't want you to feel like you've made a mistake bringing me here - I'm sorry about the door OK - listen I didn't know what I was doing - I was going through some stuff and Charlie came along - and well at the time - at the time I just followed how I was - I followed my feelings - and maybe the situation wasn't what I thought it was - and I do feel bad about it I do - and Charlie is just a complicated person OK - and you know what I'm really sorry about the door OK?

Pause.

Tom I forgive you

They smile.

Max You know I am really grateful for what you're doing for me here - I'll play by the rules

Pause.

Shall we eat or?

Max *goes over to* **Tom** *to take the shopping off him.*

Tom Just remember this time to not burn the pan - it's harder for you to wash

Max Sure

Tom And you used a bit too much oil last night - the dinner was pretty smothered in it

Max Yep

Max *starts to go towards the kitchen.*

Pause.

Tom You know saving you - taking you with me up here - I feel like it means that all that pain - it feels like that all has meaning now

Max OK

Tom That this forgiveness - is like an action - that it's tangible because in some roundabout way I'm saving you right now from - well I guess a lot of things

Pause.

Max Sounds scary out there

Tom You deserve better than him - you know that?

Pause.

Max Let's just - start again

Tom You'll get through this - I promise

Scene Three

The Cabin. A week later. Late afternoon.

Max *and* **Tom** *sit on the floor.*

Candles and esoteric paraphernalia are spread all over the place.

Max *is reading* **Tom**'s *tarot.*

Max Alright so the first card on the left is your past - it represents an idea or situation you've found yourself in, or you've been struggling with - the middle card is your present, what action you may or may not be taking now - and the end card on the right is your future, your potential, the outcome, or your aspiration

Tom Right

Max Tom

Tom Yes?

Max You said you'd take this seriously

Tom I am

Max Then watch your tone you know

Tom Sorry

Max I find this important

Tom But I just don't think that any of it is –

Max Please - I need this

Pause.

Max *turns over the cards.*

He begins to examine them, with a lot of expression.

Gasps, intrigue, shock, nodding.

Tom *watches him and rolls his eyes.*

Tom   What does it say then - go on - tell me my fortune

Max   Well your first card is Death

Tom   Great

Max   It sounds worse than it actually is

Tom   In this situation it doesn't sound ideal to be honest

Max   Death as your first card is death of the old self - of a self that was harming you - and a rebirth into something new - rising from the ashes so to speak

Tom   Oh well when you put it as vaguely as that then

Max   Your present is the Hanged Man

Tom   Jesus Christ

Max   It means letting go - surrendering to the universe - realising a state of meditation and relinquishing control of the here and now

Tom   Have you met me?

Max   I don't pick the cards

Max *goes back to look at the third card – staring at it intently.*

But something has caught **Tom's** *eye, he's distracted.*

Max   And the third is –

Max *looks up at* **Tom**.

Tom *stops being distracted briefly.*

Max   The Magician - the ability to manifest your true desire - with hard work, imagination - to get what you want, at all costs

Max *looks back up at* **Tom**.

Tom *is fully distracted.*

Max   Tom? Are you OK?

Tom *gets up and moves across the room to where he has been looking.*

He searches for something.

Max   What's wrong?

Tom   It was here this morning

Max   What was?

Tom   It's always in that corner there

Max   Calm down a minute

Tom   Right there - I always put it right there when I come in

Max   You've lost something –

Tom   The axe

Pause.

Max   Well what did you do with it this morning?

Tom   I haven't used it today

Max   But you said you saw it this morning

Tom   I always check

Max   Every morning?

Tom *stops.*

Tom   Because - well to be safe

Max   You were always a real checker

Tom   Don't start

Tom *continues searching.*

Max *packs up the tarot, watching as* **Tom** *keeps looking frantically around.*

Until **Tom** *eventually stops.*

Tom   Have you moved it?

Max Me?

Tom You wanted to take topless photos with it

Max What would I do with an axe - you said it yourself I'd be useless –

Tom I never said that

Pause.

Max You must have misplaced it somewhere - think - what did you do today?

Tom Well I went out to get food didn't I

Max Sure you didn't take the axe with you?

Tom I wouldn't take the axe out to go shopping

Max You might have taken the axe out to fetch wood and then go –

Tom My brain's fuzzy from this place –

Max Tell me exactly what you do when you go shopping

Tom Well I go down this hill we're on - but it's hard to see because of the suit

Max Right

Tom And you follow the area where it looks like there aren't as many trees like a clearing

Max I'm trying to visualise

Tom And there's been enough fallen trees in that clearing to last us - so I usually take some of that - or chop some bigger chunks up

Max OK and when do you get to the road where we parked the car when we first got here?

Tom There's a path which leads further down –

Max And you go down the path and then there's the car?

Tom *looks at* **Max**.

Max And I imagine that's the start of the road - down to the town - that's just well - I suppose that's what I'm imagining - and how long's the road - I mean just in case it's fallen somewhere or? I'm just trying to retrace your steps as much as possible - just so we both have a clear picture about where it could have gone

Pause.

Tom The questions

Max I'm trying to help you retrace –

Tom I didn't take the axe shopping - and the axe is now gone - it's either here - or in the woods

Max I was trying to help you remember

Tom And we're the only two people here

Max So you do think - what - that I'm hiding the axe from you as what some sort of joke or –

Tom *looks at* **Max**, *trying to work out what's going on.*

Max *stands there uncomfortably.*

Tom Have you - have you been outside?

Max Where have you got that from?

Pause.

Tom Are you –

Max I haven't been outside

Pause.

Tom Max if you've been outside you have to tell me - you might have exposed us - we're a team

Pause.

Has someone else been here?

Max Sorry?

Tom Have you seen –

Max No - no I haven't seen anyone there's been no one else here –

Tom Sure?

Max Yes

Tom It's either lost or someone has it

Pause.

Max It'll be in the woods then

Tom Must be huh

Max You're currently a magician so can't you magic the axe back here?

The joke doesn't go down well.

Has there been any more news

Tom It's the same no changes

Max So everyone's still in their houses

Tom If I had updates I'd tell you

Max Are people still looting?

Tom Yes - they are so

Max No changes

Tom You don't think that one of them –

Max No - I don't - I think you must have left it in the woods at some point

Pause.

Max *walks around the room to clear his head.*

Max Tom - I've been stuck in here now - for a whole month –

Tom You've done so well though

Max I don't need that

Pause.

Tom What's gotten into your head now?

Pause.

Max That it's not that bad out there

Pause.

Tom What is this?

Max How bad is it out there - give me something

Tom Well people are dying

Max How many?

Tom Thousands

Max But how do you know?

Tom Because I've seen it

Max And what does it do to them - the virus

Tom Why do you need all this –

Max I need more information Tom

Tom It's deadly

Max Yes OK it's deadly - you tell me it's deadly

Tom Because it is

Max But give me something else

Tom Like what?

Max How do they die?

Tom Horribly

Pause.

Max Why should I believe you if you can never give me a straight answer?

Tom It starts off slow - a cough - feeling tired and then a fever - and then it progresses until they start wheezing - and then they can't breathe - and they start bleeding from the inside - and blood comes from their mouths - and you choke on it - that amount of blood you choke on - either from being too weak or just the sheer volume of it

Pause.

Max Do you want to get me back - is that what this is?

Tom Are you serious?

Max Answer the question

Tom People are dying –

Max You're avoiding –

Tom You rang me up - you were the one who rang me up - and made me leave my parents behind in the city

Pause.

Max Do you want me on my own?

Tom Jesus listen to yourself

Max Is this all just some big plot to cut me off from –

Tom You're going nuts - I didn't realise, but now –

Max If it is then you have to tell me now

Tom You don't want me - you made that clear - you don't want me back - so why would I waste my time trying to do something like that? Do you think I'm insane?

Pause.

You think what that I've dragged you up here, to the middle of a bloody forest - middle of nowhere - for weeks - and lied this whole time - just me and you - like this - this tense - all to get back with you? To get back with someone who doesn't want me? Have you heard how absolutely insane that is?

Pause.

Tom I hated you - like really hated you - for a while - for what you did to me

Max You said you forgave me

Tom Forgiving someone is a process

Max So you don't then

Tom You hurt me - you - you were the one who hurt me - not the other way round

Max You weren't perfect either and you know that - you didn't let me go out

Tom That's nonsense

Max We stayed in - we didn't see friends - you didn't even go to my best friend's wedding

Tom I wasn't invited

Max Yes you were

Tom Not from her directly

Max You obsessed that I was going to leave you for somebody else

Tom And you did

Max Because I couldn't take you anymore

Pause.

Tom Right, you know what - I can't do this - get out

Max What?

Tom I've risked my life for you - my parents - and all for this - for you - and you know - this - I can't do this anymore

Max Just wait a second

Tom Accusing me of keeping you captive –

Max I didn't necessarily - let's just talk about this

Tom When I've saved your life - I've saved your life

Max I just need you to prove to me that this is real

Tom Get out - go - go on - leave - get out Max - get out

Pause.

Max *debates going.*

He looks at the door, and then back at **Tom**.

Max No

Tom *sits down.*

He starts to cry.

Tom My mum is –

Max We don't know –

Tom Dying

Max What?

Tom Which means Dad will - he'll catch it from her too

Pause.

Max Listen OK - I believe you

Tom I don't think I can do this much longer

Max *goes over to* **Tom** *to comfort him.*

Max I just - I want to help

Pause.

Let me go outside - I'll wear the suit - we just need to change the dynamic a little bit I think that will really help - you need to let me go outside - be a team

Pause.

Tom OK - you're right OK

Max Yeah?

Tom Wear the suit - go pick up supplies - share the load I suppose - they'll just think it's me hopefully

Max OK - right OK then

Pause.

Tom Max - are you sure no one else has been here?

Max Yeah

Tom Because now is the time to tell me if you've seen someone - it's about honesty

Pause.

Max It's just been us

Tom Me and you

Max Just me and you

The wind blows loudly at the door.

They both look towards it.

Scene Four

The Cabin. The next day. Midday.

The door is wide open.
It blows wildly in the wind.

Max You're gonna need to leave

Charlie Upset I found you then

Max You've left the door wide open

Charlie You're a big boy - close it

Pause.

Charlie *is in between* **Max** *and the door.*
A stand-off.

Max You're probably crawling with stuff from outside

Charlie Push me out the door then go on

Max I can't touch you

Charlie Don't want me to touch you?

Pause.

It's nice to see you

Charlie *closes the door and moves further into the cabin.*
He looks around the place.
Inspecting, checking for a bit of dust, he's not that impressed.
Before finally sitting down, and making himself at home.

Jesus imagine having sex on this

Max How did you find where I was?

Charlie How d'you think?

Pause.

I've been staying in a B and B

Max They're open?

Charlie Would you have sex on this sofa?

Max That's dangerous

Charlie You miss me?

Pause.

Come here babe come on

Charlie *stands up and goes towards* **Max**.

Max Stop

Charlie *stops.*

He laughs.

Charlie Seriously?

Max Listen I came here because I panicked - about the virus - what's been going on and so I called Tom - and you know how I panic - and he's usually right about things - so I came here with him - I took my chances and yeah so maybe I was selfish in doing that but I did it so I'm here now

Pause.

Charlie Could have called to lemme know babe

Max There's no signal here

Charlie Before you decided to become hobbits of the shire in here

Charlie *starts to walk around the cabin, looking at things.*

So are you two?

Charlie *insinuates intimacy with his fingers.*

Max No

Charlie That what this is?

Max It's nothing like that

Charlie But you're here with him aren't you

Max I told you I panicked

Charlie For all you know you left me in the city

Max But you're here

Charlie For all you know I'm trapped in the city alone - or dead

Max I didn't think you'd be dead

Charlie But you didn't know

Max Well why aren't you in the city?

Charlie I followed you guys here

Pause.

Scared?

Max No

Charlie This place is very very remote you know

Max Well it has to be - it's safe here - we're safe here from the outside and –

Charlie I want to kiss you - and you want to kiss me too - since I walked in - can feel it

Pause.

Max We're in a very dangerous situation at the moment

Charlie I think you might be yeah

Max The world I mean

Pause.

Charlie What exactly has he told you?

Pause.

You're all the way up here - just you and him - for a whole month - no one knows you're here except for me but you didn't know that - and your phone doesn't work - sound clever to you?

Max I understand you think something is going on but it isn't

Charlie But you did leave me

Pause.

I love you - so much - we're made for each other you know - you do know that - I've told you before - that's why I do so much for you - and put up with all the shit you pull

Pause.

Max OK listen I suppose we can make this work - you're going to need to shower and destroy your clothes - or we might have to keep you in the other room for a week or so - isolate you from us but I suppose yes it can work –

Charlie You're usually smarter than this - think about what he's like

Max OK stop talking to me like that - I'm trying to work out what to do in this situation

Charlie You were getting much better at handling yourself

Max Don't do that

Charlie But I can see you're scared again

Pause.

You think he has this all under control

Max It's not about that - I've already said

Charlie I won't survive without you - and you won't survive without me either

Max I'm surviving right now actually so –

Charlie With someone else

Pause.

Max This thing is big - it's getting bigger every day

Charlie What exactly do you think the situation is?

Max Well - the virus

Charlie The virus

Max It's dangerous - in the cities it's - it's gotten more contagious and –

Charlie How contagious is it?

Max It travels on the wind

Charlie The wind?

Max You've probably let a whole bunch of it in coming through the door

Charlie I'm covered in it aren't I

Max You could be

Charlie *takes his T-shirt off.*

Charlie This T-shirt? Covered in it

He throws the T-shirt towards **Max**.

Pause.

Charlie *moves towards* **Max** *again.*

Max Don't - just - stop

Charlie *laughs.*

Charlie It's over - it wasn't even that bad - it peaked - quickly actually - and now it's just the run of the mill kind of thing

Pause.

Max Well I'm sorry you think that but –

Charlie That's not what he's said has he

Pause.

Have you been outside?

Max Not yet

Charlie See?

Max But I'll wear a suit

Charlie Virus extremists - paranoid people do paranoid things

Pause.

You believe him?

Max Tell me why I should believe you?

Charlie I don't lie

Max You're the one who's been stalking us

Charlie *I've* been stalking you?

Max Up here haven't you

Charlie I love you

Pause.

You're feeling weak now aren't you - like you've made a mistake

Pause.

He wants you

Max He's very obviously moved on

Charlie He's obsessed with you come on

Max He wants a child now for Christ sake - he told me

Charlie You've let him own you again

Pause.

I forgive you - look we can work through this - come back with me now - we can forget this and move forward

Max   There's nothing to forgive

Charlie   Now I'm giving you a chance here - I really shouldn't actually - I mean I really shouldn't because you've been so - but this is your chance to make everything go back to normal and reverse all the damage you've done

Pause.

Max   No

Charlie   Come here come on

Max   I'm not going with you

Charlie   Tom is lying to you and if you'd leave this cabin you'd see for yourself

Max   I don't want to go anywhere

Charlie   You've been weak - don't be more

Max   I don't want to be with you anymore

Pause.

I don't want to be with you anymore Charlie

Charlie *stands there stunned.*

He breathes heavily.

He's getting angrier and angrier.

Until he starts hitting himself in the head.

Charlie   Stupid, stupid

Then he starts to bolt over to **Max**.

It looks like he's about to hit **Max**.

Max   Charlie stop

Charlie *stands there.*

Until he falls to his knees on the floor.

Max   Listen I'm sorry I –

Charlie   This is what you do to people - this - this is what you do - this is what loving you does to people

Charlie *starts to cry.*

Max   I'm sorry - please don't - please don't do that

Charlie   I hate you - I hate you for what you've done to me - you need me –

Max   I don't need you

Pause.

Charlie   You deserve everything that's coming to you

Pause.

I'll always love you

Scene Five

The Cabin. The next day. Night.

There is a rumble of thunder and flashes of lightning throughout.

Tom *is in an apron and busy setting the table.*

Placemats, plates, cutlery, he even lights a few candles.

There is a knock at the door.

Tom *moves to the other side of the room.*

Tom   It's open - I'm nowhere near

A man opens the door.

He is in a hazmat suit, some shopping, and quickly comes in before shutting the door behind him.

Standing there, motionless, while **Tom** *looks at him.*

Max?

Pause.

Max you're safe in here

Pause.

You can take off the mask now

Pause.

What's the matter?

Max *takes off his mask.*

He's shocked.

Tom   You're home

Pause.

This storm was unexpected

Pause.

So you've seen now

Max I did

Tom It's –

Max Yeah

Pause.

Sorry I'm actually getting quite –

Max *begins to cry.*

Tom I'm sorry

Max *continues to cry.*

Max Everyone is scared of each other - I tried to say hello to someone and they practically levitated off the ground

Tom Trauma - and a stressful situation for everyone

Pause.

Tom *puts on some rubber gloves from his pocket.*

Tom *goes towards* **Max**.

Tom Well take off the suit and –

Max No - I - I'm –

Tom OK

Max *sits down.*

Max *is still crying.*

Tom I made some dinner - I actually quite enjoyed it - you're right it was good to switch it up a bit

Max The suits are –

Tom They're necessary - to protect you - why don't you take it off now you're inside?

Scene Five 47

Max No

Tom We need to disinfect it as soon as possible

Max Sorry - I'm just feeling –

Pause.

I saw a whole family - a mum and a dad - and two little children - in little tiny suits - just like me and - masks and - it was so quiet - and when you did see people they jumped out of your way - and then that made me feel like I needed to jump out of their way –

Max *begins to cry again.*

Tom Let's just get some food in you - get you warm - you're shocked

Tom *goes to get some food.*

Pause.

Max Thank you

Tom *stops what he's doing.*

Tom What's that?

Max Thank you - for helping me

Tom That's OK

Tom *goes back to fetching the food.*

Max *starts to take off the suit.*

Tom I'm glad you've seen - in a way I'm glad you've seen for yourself - just how mad it is out there - and it just goes to show how safe we are up here - actually how lucky we are

Tom *hands* **Max** *a bowl of food.*

Max Do you want to sit at the table?

Tom It's OK

Max I feel bad

Tom Nothing to feel bad about

Pause.

Max I don't want to go out - anymore - I don't think I can do that again

Tom OK

Max I think I'll just stay in here

Tom That's OK - that's totally OK

Tom *places his hand on* **Max**'s *knee.*

Pause.

Tom *starts to eat.*

Max Why did you save me?

Tom You asked me to

Pause.

Instinct - my instinct told me I had to save you

Pause.

I'm just glad you're safe now

Max In here yeah - but –

Tom You'll survive - you'll survive this - I promised

A flash of lightning is seen.

Tom *gets back to eating.*

A rumble of thunder is heard.

Max I'm sorry I left you

Tom We don't have to talk about that

Max In that way - I'm sorry I left you in that way

Tom I forgive you

Max For real this time?

Tom Absolutely

Pause.

I'm glad to see you're feeling better about staying here with me

Max I want to stay here, inside here, forever, I don't want to go out and see that kind of a world ever again - seeing those children in their suits

Tom Aren't they sweet?

Max No it's –

Tom Scary you're right - sorry I was just trying to lighten the mood

Max I understand

Tom They're just so tiny and - sometimes it looks so sweet

Pause.

They eat.

Another flash of lightning.

Max When we were together - did you know you wanted children?

Tom I did

Max You wanted us to have a family?

Pause.

Another rumble of thunder.

You didn't tell me

Tom There wasn't the right time

Pause.

Max And do you still?

Tom I want kids yeah

Max With me?

Max *puts down his bowl and takes* **Tom**'s *bowl too.*

They stare at each other for a moment.

Then **Max** *takes* **Tom** *by the hand.*

Max We can start again

Tom Max what are you doing?

Max You'd planned the future?

Tom I'm the organised one - although I hadn't counted on what kind of a world it would become

Max Yeah

Pause.

I think - I think I would have loved to have a baby –

Pause.

Tom When you left I was heartbroken

Max So was I

Tom I couldn't imagine life without you there - so when this happened I –

Max *kisses* **Tom**.

Tom *pulls away.*

Tom Max I can't

Max Why not?

Tom What about Charlie?

Max Screw Charlie

Tom Max I don't want to get hurt again

Max You won't

Tom It nearly destroyed me

Max I want you

Pause.

They look at each other.

Tom Really?

Max *nods.*

Pause.

Tom *kisses* **Max**.

The kiss grows.

There is a flash of lightning, really close to the cabin now, and it illuminates the window at the back, to reveal the silhouette of a man standing outside.

Watching them kiss.

A rumble of thunder is heard right overhead.

Scene Six

The Cabin. The next day. Midday.

Charlie *is holding the axe.*

The door is open.

Charlie   Well well well - didn't expect it to be you here

Tom   Get out

Charlie   No

Tom   If you don't leave I'll –

Charlie   Shall I shut the door?

Tom   I'll call the police

Charlie   No signal up here

Pause.

Not happy to see me then?

Tom   I knew you were here - I could feel it

Charlie   Where is he?

Charlie *closes the door.*

Nice cabin

Tom   Put the axe down

Charlie   Rustic isn't it

Tom   Let's talk

Charlie   Knew you had rich parents

Tom   Or give it to me

Charlie   Narcissistic little rich boy

Tom   You've been stalking us?

Charlie Yeah I have

Tom You're the one who –

Charlie Took a leaf out of your book - I've seen you chopping wood - go to the shops - take the car - I've watched you - just like you

Pause.

Tom I don't know what you mean

Charlie You're fucking insane aren't you

Tom You're the one camping outside - stalking his own boyfriend - and wielding an axe

Charlie That is you - I'm not insane that is you

Pause.

Tom Just put the axe down so we can talk

Charlie OK stop acting like I'm being crazy

Pause.

This you trying to steal him back?

Tom Listen to yourself

Charlie I'm in love - in actual love with him

Pause.

Do you think I haven't spotted you - hiding outside our flat - calling me repeatedly from an unknown number - breathing heavily down the phone - I've seen you outside my work - I bet you also go to his

Tom You've lost it –

Charlie Don't try that with me

Pause.

Charlie *begins to cough - he tries to stifle it with his mouth and hands.*

Tom *watches.*

The cough goes on.

And on.

And on.

The cough subsides.

Charlie It's over - accept it - I won

Tom Nothing's over

Pause.

Charlie Did you think you were going to live out here - in this fucking cabin - until what - you guys got back together?

Tom I needed to get him away from you

Charlie What happens after - you stay here forever?

Tom Violent domestic abuser - that's what you are

Charlie Live out some weird woodland fantasy?

Tom A fucking brute - and a coward for doing that

Charlie I'm the one with the fucking axe mate

Pause.

Tom I couldn't see someone I love go through that

Charlie Someone you love

Tom Exactly

Charlie Sure he had a great life with you

Tom He did actually

Charlie Then why did he pick me?

Pause.

Tom He's too easy to lead - he doesn't think - never did

Charlie Cos he didn't want a computer nerd for a boyfriend

Tom Shut up

Charlie I've heard all about you - from him - stopping him seeing friends - blocking family members on his phone - kept him tucked away like a little pet - your little prize was he - cos you couldn't imagine him staying with a guy like you

Tom He's not your possession you know

Charlie Even changed the locks once - literally tried locking him away already - that didn't work - that just made - had to think of something different - and you've created the same situation here - because you're a small little –

Tom He is mine

Pause.

Tom *is shocked with his outburst.*

Charlie *smiles.*

Pause.

Charlie He chose me - he left you for me –

Tom Looks like he's picked me now –

Charlie And he'll do it again once this is all over

Pause.

You think he's picked you for real? You really think he's picked you?

Charlie *laughs at* **Tom**.

He goes to put the axe down.

He takes a seat - still chuckling to himself.

Charlie I saw him already - but he didn't tell you that obviously - he tried to kiss me

Tom He didn't

Charlie I told him he'd have to earn me back

Tom You're lying

Charlie We sat on this sofa together - he was all over me - and he begged me to take him back

Pause.

Touched a sore spot haven't I

Tom Don't believe you

Charlie He'll always want me

Pause.

The wind howls at the door and the window.

Tom *looks towards it.*

Charlie *watches him.*

Charlie The wind - I mean he seriously believed you about the wind?

Tom He believes the truth yeah

Charlie Come on now - let's get this all out in the open

Pause.

I have to admit the balls you had to try and pull this off

Tom I knew what I was doing was right

Charlie Keep telling yourself that

Tom He's not going to take you back

Charlie He's not going to take you back - not for real - you just can't see it

Tom I guess we'll see

Charlie You live in a fantasy

Tom He trusts me

Scene Six 57

Charlie I'm sure he'll trust you even more when he finds out about all of this

Tom He knows I'm good for him

Charlie That you've used all of this - to scare him - to come back to you

Tom In this situation? I don't think you'd be his first option

Charlie For what?

Tom To keep him safe - you were never much of a thinker

Pause.

Charlie *stands up.*

He's getting more agitated.

Charlie If he's not out of this cabin by this time tomorrow I'm going to the police

Tom No signal here

Charlie I'll go into town

Pause.

You've been caught - this - all this - it's a lie –

Tom You're not making any –

Charlie The virus wasn't anything - it was the flu - you've spun this web to your own advantage and now you've been caught and it's over - admit it

Tom *starts to laugh.*

The laugh grows and grows and grows.

It's more and more manic – disturbing.

Charlie What are you - stop - stop it - stop it you're acting weird

Tom Have you - have you just been going about your business?

Charlie Stop laughing - you're creeping me out

Tom Going about your business and -

Tom *continues to laugh.*

Charlie *watches him.*

Tom You've not taken it seriously? It's not a lie - I'm not lying

Charlie You are lying so

Tom I'm not - you've just been going about your business and - do you not read the news - are you that much of a Neanderthal - fuck me you're stupid

Tom *continues to laugh.*

Charlie You're talking shit

Tom I haven't made any of this up - you're right I wanted Max back - the virus hit and - and I saw an opportunity - to get him away from you - but the virus is bad it's - deadly

Charlie Virus extremism

Tom Have you not seen anyone in protective suits

Charlie I've only seen you - wearing that stupid suit from my van -

Tom You've been camping out?

Charlie My camper van yeah

Tom Oh my god -

Charlie What d'you mean?

Tom If you had bothered to go down the road and -

Charlie I have - at night - there wasn't anyone there

Pause.

Tom *You've* been looting

Charlie Not looting - borrowing - didn't want people to know I'm here - might bump into you

Tom Then you haven't seen all the people in their suits

Tom *backs away from* **Charlie** *as much as possible.*

Tom Stay away from me

Charlie Stop it

Tom You're probably covered in it

Charlie Piss off

Tom Stay away from me

Charlie I'm not playing this game with you

Charlie *moves towards* **Tom**.

Tom *clambers to get away.*

Tom You're going to die

Pause.

Charlie I haven't got any symptoms

Tom You have a cough

Charlie From being outside

Tom Exactly

Pause.

It starts to dawn on **Charlie**.

Tom There's a cough - which doesn't go away - which gets worse and harder to manage - and then you start to bleed from your insides

Charlie This is all your bullshit

Tom Have you noticed any blood?

Pause.

Tom You really are thick aren't you

Charlie Wait - what - wait - what am I going to?

Tom You need to go to hospital - now

Charlie *is stunned by this.*

He starts to breathe heavily.

Charlie If this is one of your little games I'll be back here with the police

Tom It's not

Charlie *reluctantly turns around and runs out the door.*

Tom *rushes over to lock the door behind him.*

Max *comes out of the bedroom, sleepy.*

Max Is everything OK?

Tom My love - I thought I'd locked the bedroom door

Max You did?

Tom To make sure you were resting

Max I heard noises

Tom Just talking to myself

Max About what?

Tom You know me

Max Voices

Tom You must have been dreaming

Max Sorry I've slept all day again

Tom That's OK my love

Max What time is it?

Tom That doesn't matter - if you need rest you need rest

Max I should probably get up

Tom Go back to bed babe

Max I think I've slept enough

Tom Go back to bed

Max No I should try and do something

Tom Max do as you're told

Pause.

I'm just trying to help you my love - don't take that for granted - OK?

Pause.

Max *turns around to go back to bed.*

Tom Max - why is your top off?

Max My top

Tom You know I hate it when you sleep without a top on

Max Oh

Tom Yeah?

Pause.

Max Sorry

Tom Don't forget next time

Pause.

And Max

Max Yeah?

Tom We're going to need to have sex tonight

Max Oh

Tom So you don't want to

Max No that's not what I'm saying

Tom Good - so make sure you're ready

Max But what if –

Tom I've done a lot for you - you know that

A stand-off.

Max *goes back to the bedroom.*

Tom *looks towards the front door again.*

He notices that **Max** *has left his tarot cards on the table.*

He picks them up.

In a fit of anger he starts to rip the cards in half - more and more frantically.

Until he's left standing there - panting - with the cards ripped up around him.

Scene Seven

The Cabin. The next day. Evening.

Tom *and* **Max** *are eating dessert.*

Max *is sitting there, staring into space, not eating.*

Tom *keeps looking towards the front door, anxiously, throughout.*

Max It's cold in here

Tom The wood burner is working - it's just cold out

Pause.

How's the banana bread?

Max Honestly?

Tom Honestly

Max I don't think I'll ever want to eat it again after this

Tom Charming

Max Not that yours is bad - that came out wrong

Tom I'm trying

Max I didn't mean specifically about *your* banana bread

Tom I'm sorry I'm not good enough I guess

Max I didn't say that

Tom Sounds like that's what you're saying

Pause.

Max Is something wrong?

Tom You tell me

Max If this is going to work things have to be different to last time

Pause.

You've been really tense

Tom *starts to laugh – mockingly.*

Tom And did you want to ask me why?

Max That's what I'm doing now

Tom Well about bloody time isn't it Max

Max OK what exactly do you need from me?

Tom Excuse me?

Max How can I support you right now - you're tense –

Tom You're really going to ask me how I need support? Me? Someone you know intimately, for years? You really don't have any ideas?

Max I'm trying to open a conversation

Tom Wow - really? Wow

Pause.

Anything you want to tell me?

Max No

Tom Seriously?

Pause.

Max I don't know what you mean –

Tom You've lied to me

Max I haven't

Tom Don't - make it worse

Max About what?

Tom Just admit it and we can move on

Max There's nothing to admit

Scene Seven

Tom *laughs.*

Tom Someone else has been here

Pause.

Max *goes to speak.*

Tom Don't do that

Pause.

Do you want me Max?

Max What do you mean?

Tom You said you're sorry for leaving me - because of Charlie right - you said –

Max Exactly –

Tom But did you still want me before then?

Pause.

I know this situation has forced us together right - but I'm starting to feel like you only want me again now that the world is so terrible

Pause.

Max *stands up and takes the plates away to the kitchen.*

Tom Put the bowls in the sink - I'll wash up since you're incapable of doing anything round here but sleep all day

Pause.

Max *comes back in and goes to sit on the sofa.*

Tom Max?

Max Yes?

Tom I asked you a question

Max I know

Tom Well what's the answer?

Max I don't know

Tom You don't know?

Max That's what I said

Tom Unbelievable

Max We can't just go back to how it was

Tom Last night was pathetic

Max Don't say that

Tom Or are you just not brave enough to leave

Pause.

Tom *goes to sit by* **Max**.

Tom *kisses* **Max**.

The kiss grows.

Max *isn't happy with it and pulls away.*

Tom Don't do that

Tom *grabs* **Max** *to try and kiss him.*

They struggle.

Tom *grabs* **Max**'s *hair.*

Tom *pulls at* **Max**'s *crotch.*

They struggle.

Until **Max** *bites* **Tom**'s *lip.*

Tom *gets off of* **Max**.

Max *stands up and backs away from* **Tom**.

Max Get the fuck off me

Tom You bit me

Pause.

You piece of shit

Tom *gets up.*

You're going to get yourself killed one day

Max   Don't threaten me

Tom   You're going to get your head beaten in one day do you know that?

Max   You're insane

Tom   No I'm not

Max *goes to the bedroom.*

Tom   What are you doing?

Max   Going out

Tom   It's nighttime

Max   I need a walk

Pause.

Tom   Come on Max let's talk - I didn't mean it - Max I didn't mean it - Max you have to listen to me - listen to me

Tom *is erratic and doesn't know what to do.*

Max *comes back in in the hazmat suit.*

Tom *grabs at* **Max** *to force himself on him.*

Tom   You're mine do you understand me - you're mine

Max *kicks* **Tom** *off.*

Max *grabs the axe.*

Tom   Oh what are you going to do with that then?

Max   Stay away from me

Tom   After I've saved your life

Max   That's a warning

Tom Isn't that what you like? Don't you like it rough - isn't that why you left - you take it from Charlie but you won't take it from me?

Max I'm not with Charlie anymore because he does exactly that to me

Tom You don't want me? Don't find me sexy? Is that it? Would I be more sexy if I was beating your head in every day?

Max I don't want anyone

The door bursts open.

Charlie *is there.*

He's even more erratic than usual but quite weak.

Tom Stay back

Charlie It's a trap

Tom Don't go near him - don't touch him

Max What's wrong with him?

Tom He has it

Charlie Stay away from him

Tom Charlie you need to leave - you'll kill us

Charlie He's trapped you

Tom He'll kill us

Charlie I love you Max

Pause.

Charlie *is wheezing.*

Max Charlie what's happened?

Max *goes towards* **Charlie**.

Tom Don't go near him

Max *stops.*

Charlie Max - I love you and - I needed to tell you that one last time

Tom He doesn't love you - what we had was love –

Charlie He'll be the end of you

Max You both keep saying that –

Charlie Max I'm dying - I'm going to die

Max What?

Max *starts to go to* **Charlie**.

Tom Stop - we need to get him out of here he'll infect both of us

Max *stops abruptly.*

Tom I told you to go to the hospital

Max You were here with him?

Tom I was trying to save his life

Max Lies - Tom - lies were a big thing for us

Charlie I went - I did - as fast as I could - and when I got there they were all in suits - those fucking suits and they wanted to restrain me - got out all this gear to almost tie me up - you told me they'd help me - hospitals help people but not this one - and I wasn't going to stay there and wait - and just wait for it to - to - so I smashed the place up - completely wrecked the place - and I drove as fast as I could away from there - and then I had this instinct to just - I came back here - something was telling me to come back here so I could be with you

Pause.

Tom I was trying to help him - and now he's come back to infect us both

Charlie I needed to see you

Pause.

You don't have to go back to him - you don't - you can - Max I love you

Tom Don't touch him - he's trying to kill you - if he can't have you then no one can that's what he wants

Pause.

Max If you loved me - then why - why did you hurt me

Charlie Because –

Max Why did you used to hit me –

Charlie Because I –

Max I ended up in hospital

Charlie *gets angry and steps towards* **Max**, *aggressively.*

Charlie Because you drove me crazy

Max *takes a step back.*

Charlie *realises what he's done.*

Tom See? You left me for this

Charlie He's been stalking us - for months - he waits outside our door - for months - at your work, at mine –

Tom He's lying

Max You were the one stalking us this whole time?

Tom I'm not obsessed with you no

Charlie He's made you think you don't have any options - this is a trap

Tom My parents might be out there dying right now for all we know - and I chose you –

Max I thought your mum already was?

Tom I never said that

Max Yes you did

Tom I didn't

Max You said your mum had caught the virus and it wouldn't be long until your dad did too

Pause.

Tom Max don't be stupid - you have a choice now - to start again with me here - you can't do this by yourself look at you - think about it - it's scary out there - think about those kids in the suits - you won't manage - you wouldn't have survived without me - he's trying to kill you - don't be stupid

Pause.

Max Do you love me Charlie?

Charlie Yes

Max How much?

Charlie I had to see you one last time

Tom He doesn't love you - that's the whole point - he just wants to hurt you - I loved you - real love - and you loved me - you wouldn't still be here if you didn't still - and I have saved you - look around I have saved you Max - and I won't ever stop loving you Max you know - I won't - I won't ever stop loving you you have my word

Max I don't want you - I don't - I don't want anyone

Pause.

Tom You can leave if you want but I'll find you - I have to save you - I wouldn't hurt you - and I will always be there for you - loving you - I'll always be there - so just accept it - just accept that you need me - accept that - because I'm not going away - I will never go away - I will find you - always - I will always be there in the background because you need me - and you're going to need me in the end

Pause.

Max *puts on the protective mask.*

Max *moves towards* **Charlie**.

Tom Stop –

Max *points the axe at* **Tom**.

Tom *stops.*

Max *goes closer to* **Charlie**.

He puts out his hand and touches his face.

It is tender.

Max *hands* **Charlie** *the axe.*

Charlie *takes the axe.*

Max *steps away from* **Charlie** *and takes off his mask.*

Max I'm not stupid I'm scared - I'm not selfish - I've always just been scared - of everything - worried about what if, what happens when, what if that happens and then this happens and that happens over there - what if I miss the train, what if the cat throws up from eating something bad and then dies, what if I get hit by a bus and what happens to the bus driver who kills me, does he then live his life in total utter misery? What if they laugh at me and then I can't get out of bed ever again because they've laughed at me, what if the air is poison, what if I forget how to swim, what if I'm in the sun too long and a cancer makes a nest in my skin, above the ankle and it slowly over a period of years hatches and crawls its way up and takes over my entire body, what if I don't pay that bill and all the others, open that door, eat that food, wear those clothes, say those things, breathe that amount of times and that worry - that being scared - all the time - that being scared all the time has gotten me nowhere - it has given me nothing - it has given me you two - you two who never stop - and now look where we are - at the end of the fucking world and I have you two standing right in front of me - and I don't actually give a fuck anymore, I don't care if I live or die, I just refuse to live the rest of my time on this planet in a state of total fucking fear - fear that both of you have filled me with - poisoned me with - over the years - because if I die now, tomorrow, next month or next year - it'll be without either of you

Pause.

Max *puts his mask back on.*

Tom   No hang on - wait - just hang on just - where are you going - just wait a second Max I love you

Tom *goes towards* **Max** *but* **Charlie** *gets in his way.*

There is a stand off, as **Charlie** *points the axe at* **Tom***.*

Tom   That's the only suit - you can't leave with the only suit - you wouldn't survive without me - think about the world out there think about how scary the world is out there Max right now - just think about how totally and utterly terrifying it is out there right now Max and just - and just stop - please just stop

Pause.

Max *leaves.*

Charlie *and* **Tom** *stand there – facing each other.*

Charlie *raises the axe.*

Scene Eight

The Cabin. The next day. Morning.

Morning light streaks in from the window.
Tom, *and only* **Tom**, *lies dead on the floor.*
Motionless.
The wind howls outside.
The door swings in the wind.
And the wind comes in and fills the room.

Discover. Read. Listen. Watch.

A NEW WAY TO ENGAGE WITH PLAYS

This award-winning digital library features over 3,000 playtexts, 400 audio plays, 300 hours of video and 360 scholarly books.

Playtexts published by Methuen Drama, The Arden Shakespeare, Faber & Faber, Playwrights Canada Press, Aurora Metro Books and Nick Hern Books.

Audio Plays from L.A. Theatre Works featuring classic and modern works from the oeuvres of leading American playwrights.

Video collections including films of live performances from the RSC, The Globe and The National Theatre, as well as acting masterclasses and BBC feature films and documentaries.

FIND OUT MORE:
www.dramaonlinelibrary.com • @dramaonlinelib

Methuen Drama Modern Plays

include

Bola Agbaje
Edward Albee
Ayad Akhtar
Jean Anouilh
John Arden
Peter Barnes
Sebastian Barry
Clare Barron
Alistair Beaton
Brendan Behan
Edward Bond
William Boyd
Bertolt Brecht
Howard Brenton
Amelia Bullmore
Anthony Burgess
Leo Butler
Jim Cartwright
Lolita Chakrabarti
Caryl Churchill
Lucinda Coxon
Tim Crouch
Shelagh Delaney
Ishy Din
Claire Dowie
David Edgar
David Eldridge
Dario Fo
Michael Frayn
John Godber
James Graham
David Greig
John Guare
Lauren Gunderson
Peter Handke
David Harrower
Jonathan Harvey
Robert Holman
David Ireland
Sarah Kane
Barrie Keeffe
Jasmine Lee-Jones
Anders Lustgarten
Duncan Macmillan
David Mamet
Patrick Marber
Martin McDonagh
Arthur Miller
Alistair McDowall
Tom Murphy
Phyllis Nagy
Anthony Neilson
Peter Nichols
Ben Okri
Joe Orton
Vinay Patel
Joe Penhall
Luigi Pirandello
Stephen Poliakoff
Lucy Prebble
Peter Quilter
Mark Ravenhill
Philip Ridley
Willy Russell
Jackie Sibblies Drury
Sam Shepard
Martin Sherman
Chris Shinn
Wole Soyinka
Simon Stephens
Kae Tempest
Anne Washburn
Laura Wade
Theatre Workshop
Timberlake Wertenbaker
Roy Williams
Snoo Wilson
Frances Ya-Chu Cowhig
Benjamin Zephaniah

Methuen Drama Contemporary Dramatists

include

John Arden (two volumes)
Arden & D'Arcy
Peter Barnes (three volumes)
Sebastian Barry
Mike Bartlett
Clare Barron
Brad Birch
Dermot Bolger
Edward Bond (ten volumes)
Howard Brenton (two volumes)
Leo Butler (two volumes)
Richard Cameron
Jim Cartwright
Caryl Churchill (two volumes)
Complicite
Sarah Daniels (two volumes)
Nick Darke
David Edgar (three volumes)
David Eldridge (two volumes)
Ben Elton
Per Olov Enquist
Dario Fo (two volumes)
Michael Frayn (four volumes)
John Godber (four volumes)
Paul Godfrey
James Graham (two volumes)
David Greig
John Guare
Lee Hall (two volumes)
Katori Hall
Peter Handke
Jonathan Harvey (two volumes)
Iain Heggie
Israel Horovitz
Declan Hughes
Terry Johnson (three volumes)
Sarah Kane
Barrie Keeffe
Bernard-Marie Koltès (two volumes)
Franz Xaver Kroetz
Kwame Kwei-Armah
David Lan
Bryony Lavery
Deborah Levy
Doug Lucie

Alistair MacDowall
Sabrina Mahfouz
David Mamet (six volumes)
Patrick Marber
Martin McDonagh
Duncan McLean
David Mercer (two volumes)
Anthony Minghella (two volumes)
Rory Mullarkey
Tom Murphy (six volumes)
Phyllis Nagy
Anthony Neilson (three volumes)
Peter Nichol (two volumes)
Philip Osment
Gary Owen
Louise Page
Stewart Parker (two volumes)
Joe Penhall (two volumes)
Stephen Poliakoff (three volumes)
David Rabe (two volumes)
Mark Ravenhill (three volumes)
Christina Reid
Philip Ridley (two volumes)
Willy Russell
Eric-Emmanuel Schmitt
Ntozake Shange
Sam Shepard (two volumes)
Martin Sherman (two volumes)
Christopher Shinn (two volumes)
Joshua Sobel
Wole Soyinka (two volumes)
Simon Stephens (five volumes)
Shelagh Stephenson
David Storey (three volumes)
C. P. Taylor
Sue Townsend
Judy Upton (two volumes)
Michel Vinaver (two volumes)
Arnold Wesker (two volumes)
Peter Whelan
Michael Wilcox
Roy Williams (four volumes)
David Williamson
Snoo Wilson (two volumes)
David Wood (two volumes)
Victoria Wood

Methuen Drama Student Editions

Alan Ayckbourn *Confusions* • **Mike Bartlett** *Earthquakes in London* • **Aphra Behn** *The Rover* • **Alice Birch** *Revolt. She Said. Revolt Again* • **Edward Bond** *Lear* • *Saved* • **Bertolt Brecht** *The Caucasian Chalk Circle* • *Fear and Misery in the Third Reich* • *The Good Person of Szechwan* • *Life of Galileo* • *Mother Courage and her Children* • *The Resistible Rise of Arturo Ui* • *The Threepenny Opera* • **Jon Brittain** *Rotterdam* • **Georg Büchner** *Woyzeck* • **Anton Chekhov** *The Cherry Orchard* • *The Seagull* • *Three Sisters* • *Uncle Vanya* • **Caryl Churchill** *Serious Money* • *Top Girls* • **Shelagh Delaney** *A Taste of Honey* • **Inua Ellams** *Barber Shop Chronicles* • **Euripides** *Elektra* • *Medea* • **Dario Fo** *Accidental Death of an Anarchist* • **Michael Frayn** *Copenhagen* • **John Galsworthy** *Strife* • **Nikolai Gogol** *The Government Inspector* • **Carlo Goldoni** *A Servant to Two Masters* • **James Graham** *This House* • **Tanika Gupta** *The Empress* • **Katori Hall** *The Mountaintop* • **Lorraine Hansberry** *A Raisin in the Sun* • **Robert Holman** *Across Oka* • **Henrik Ibsen** *A Doll's House* • *Ghosts* • *Hedda Gabler* • **Sarah Kane** *4.48 Psychosis* • *Blasted* • **Charlotte Keatley** *My Mother Said I Never Should* • **Dennis Kelly** *DNA* • **Bernard Kops** *Dreams of Anne Frank* • **Federico García Lorca** *Blood Wedding* • *Doña Rosita the Spinster* (bilingual edition) • *The House of Bernarda Alba* (bilingual edition) • *Yerma* (bilingual edition) • **David Mamet** *Glengarry Glen Ross* • *Oleanna* • **Patrick Marber** *Closer* • **John Marston** *The Malcontent* • **Martin McDonagh** *The Lieutenant of Inishmore* • *The Lonesome West* • *The Beauty Queen of Leenane* • *The Cripple of Inishmaan* • **Alistair McDowall** *Pomona* • **John McGrath** *The Cheviot, the Stag and the Black, Black Oil* • **Arthur Miller** *All My Sons* • *The Crucible* • *A View from the Bridge* • *Death of a Salesman* • *The Price* • *After the Fall* • *The Last Yankee* • *A Memory of Two Mondays* • *Broken Glass* • *Incident at Vichy* • *The American Clock* • *The Ride Down Mt. Morgan* • **Joe Orton** *Loot* • **Joe Penhall** *Blue/Orange* • **Luigi Pirandello** *Six Characters in Search of an Author* • **Lucy Prebble** *Enron* • **Mark Ravenhill** *Shopping and F***ing* • **Reginald Rose** *Twelve Angry Men* • **Willy Russell** *Blood Brothers* • *Educating Rita* • **Lemn Sissay** Benjamin Zephaniah's *Refugee Boy* • **Sophocles** *Antigone* • *Oedipus the King* • **Wole Soyinka** *Death and the King's Horseman* • **Simon Stephens** *Punk Rock* • *Pornography* • **Shelagh Stephenson** *The Memory of Water* • **August Strindberg** *Miss Julie* • **J. M. Synge** *The Playboy of the Western World* • **Kae Tempest** *Wasted* • **Theatre Workshop** *Oh What a Lovely War* • **Laura Wade** *Posh* • **Frank Wedekind** *Spring Awakening* • **Timberlake Wertenbaker** *Our Country's Good* • **Arnold Wesker** *The Merchant* • **Peter Whelan** *The Accrington Pals* • **Oscar Wilde** *The Importance of Being Earnest* • **Roy Williams** *Sing Yer Heart Out for the Lads* • **Tennessee Williams** *A Streetcar Named Desire* • *The Glass Menagerie* • *Cat on a Hot Tin Roof* • *Sweet Bird of Youth*

Methuen Drama World Classics
include

Jean Anouilh (two volumes)
John Arden (two volumes)
Brendan Behan
Aphra Behn
Bertolt Brecht (eight volumes)
Georg Büchner
Mikhail Bulgakov
Pedro Calderón
Karel Čapek
Peter Nichols (two volumes)
Anton Chekhov
Noël Coward (nine volumes)
Georges Feydeau (two volumes)
Eduardo De Filippo
Max Frisch (two volumes)
John Galsworthy
Nikolai Gogol (two volumes)
Maxim Gorky (two volumes)
Harley Granville Barker
(two volumes)
Victor Hugo
Henrik Ibsen (six volumes)
Alfred Jarry
Federico García Lorca
(three volumes)
Pierre Marivaux
Mustapha Matura
David Mercer
(two volumes)
Arthur Miller (six volumes)
Molière
Pierre de Musset
Joe Orton
A. W. Pinero
Luigi Pirandello
Terence Rattigan
W. Somerset Maugham
August Strindberg
(three volumes)
J. M. Synge
Ramón del Valle-Inclán
Frank Wedekind
Oscar Wilde
Tennessee Williams

Methuen Drama
Classical Greek Dramatists

Aeschylus Plays: One
(Persians, Seven Against Thebes, Suppliants,
Prometheus Bound)

Aeschylus Plays: Two
(Oresteia: Agamemnon, Libation-Bearers, Eumenides)

Aristophanes Plays: One
(Acharnians, Knights, Peace, Lysistrata)

Aristophanes Plays: Two
(Wasps, Clouds, Birds, Festival Time, Frogs)

Aristophanes & Menander: New Comedy
(Women in Power, Wealth, The Malcontent,
The Woman from Samos)

Euripides Plays: One
(Medea, The Phoenician Women, Bacchae)

Euripides Plays: Two
(Hecuba, The Women of Troy, Iphigeneia at Aulis, Cyclops)

Euripides Plays: Three
(Alkestis, Helen, Ion)

Euripides Plays: Four
(Elektra, Orestes, Iphigeneia in Tauris)

Euripides Plays: Five
(Andromache, Herakles' Children, Herakles)

Euripides Plays: Six
(Hippolytos, Suppliants, Rhesos)

Sophocles Plays: One
(Oedipus the King, Oedipus at Colonus, Antigone)

Sophocles Plays: Two
(Ajax, Women of Trachis, Electra, Philoctetes)

For a complete listing of
Methuen Drama titles, visit:
www.bloomsbury.com/drama

Follow us on Twitter and keep up to date
with our news and publications
@MethuenDrama